Raiser

# EDVARD MUNCH

## IN THE NATIONAL MUSEUM

# EDVARD MUNCH
## IN THE NATIONAL MUSEUM

Texts by:

Frithjof Bringager          FB
Frode Ernst Haverkamp       EH
Sidsel Helliesen            SH
Marit Ingeborg Lange        ML
Ellen J. Lerberg            EL
Nina Denney Ness            NDN
Møyfrid Tveit               MT
Øystein Ustvedt             ØU
Marianne Yvenes             MY

# Contents

# Preface

The National Museum's collection of paintings and works on paper by Edvard Munch contains many of the artist's most significant creations. These works, internationally the best known part of the museum's collection, came to the National Gallery (now part of the National Museum) partly through purchase and partly thanks to generous donations. The collection encompasses both early and late works from the artist's career; here we find portraits, landscapes, and motifs from the "Frieze of Life" series. The first Munch painting acquired by the National Gallery was the evocative *Night in Nice*, purchased at the National Annual Autumn Exhibition in 1891 for 200 kroner.

Collectively, the museum's Munch collection offers an excellent cross-section of the artist's development. Much of the collection is displayed in the museum's dedicated Munch room, and the number of visitors who pass through it each year is considerable.

This publication presents a selection of the museum's artworks by Edvard Munch, covering the period from the early 1880s through to 1919. Following a brief introductory article, the pictures are presented in chronological order. Finally, there is a short biography summarising important moments in Munch's life and career.

We hope this will deepen the visitor's insight into the work of a unique artist.

Audun Eckhoff
Director

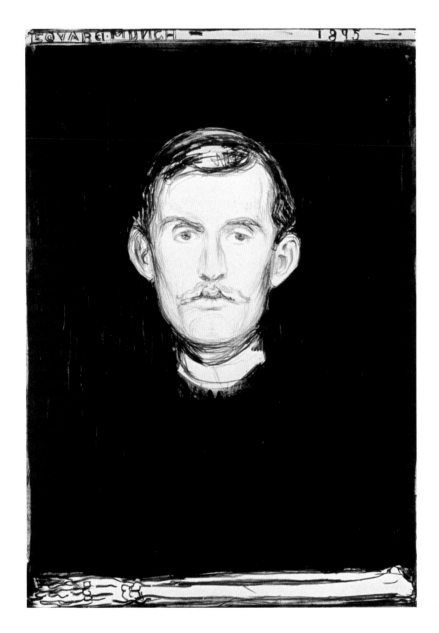

*Selv-Portrait,*
1895, lithograph,
457 x 323 mm.

# Edvard Munch

When Edvard Munch (1863–1944) was just one year old, his family moved from Løten to Christiania (Oslo). His father had been appointed doctor to an army garrison in the capital, and the family eventually moved to the newly established housing area of Grünerløkka. In 1868 Edvard's mother died, leaving five children, for whom her sister Karen Bjølstad assumed responsibility. At the age of just fifteen, Edvard's older sister Sophie died of consumption. Edvard himself was twelve at the time. The sickness and death of his mother and sister were a theme he would return to on several occasions in his work as a painter, not least in *The Sick Child* (1886) and *Death in the Sick-Room* (1893).

In 1882, during a brief period of study at the Royal School of Art and Design, Munch rented a studio with six youthful colleagues. The painter Christian Krohg, who had a studio in the same building, tutored the young artists. Munch's early works include *Andreas Reading* from 1883. The picture complies with the dogma of realism regarding precise depiction of the world and the equal legitimacy of all kinds of motifs. Here we see the artist's brother bent over a book. The choice of motif and its treatment echo the art of Krohg. During this period, Munch also frequented the circle around Hans Jæger, which was known as the Christiania Bohemians. This was a group of young intellectuals, writers and painters who were opposed to what they regarded as the double moral standards of bourgeois society. In addition to Jæger and Krohg, Munch also became acquainted with Sigbjørn Obstfelder, Oda Engelhart (who later married Krohg), Gunnar Heiberg and Jappe Nilssen.

In 1885 Munch travelled to Paris for the first time. Having participated in his first exhibition outside Norway, the World Exhibition in Antwerp, he visited the major museums and galleries of the great metropolis. Significant encounters with the period's modern painters and works by old masters made a deep impression on him. In 1889 he returned to Paris, where he spent some months studying under Léon Bonnat. In the meantime he had stirred considerable interest in Norwegian art circles by showing his painting *The Sick Child* at the National Annual Autumn Exhibition in 1886. The picture was widely commented on and discussed in the daily papers.

*Andreas Reading,* (1883), oil on cardboard, 51.5 x 35.5 cm.

*Study for a Portrait*, 1887, oil on canvas, 25.5 x 29 cm. For this study Munch may have used the same model that he used the previous year, in *The Sick Child*.

Having been invited to mount a solo exhibition at the Verein Berliner Künstler in autumn 1892, Munch travelled to Berlin. There he quickly became part of the group that met at the café-bar "Zum schwarzen Ferkel", where the tone was largely set by the Swedish writer and painter August Strindberg and the Polish poet Stanislav Przybyszewski. Others whom Munch met in this circle were Sigbjørn Obstfelder, Gustav Vigeland and the beautiful sisters Dagny and Ragnhild Juel (Dagny would later marry Przybyszewski, Ragnhild the Swedish professor and politician Helge Bäckström). Intellectual interests in the 1890s revolved around the life of the spirit, mysticism, the position of women in society, and the relation between the sexes, all of which were reflected in the work of the Ferkel artists.

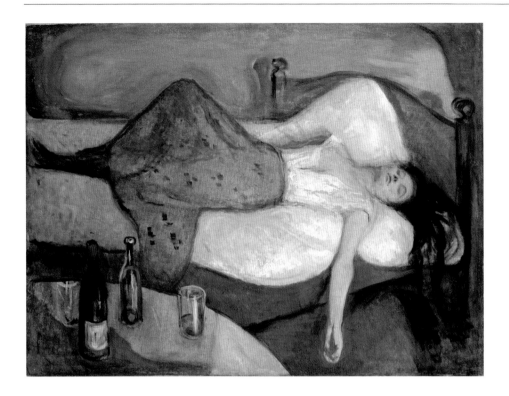

Munch's exhibition at the Verein Berliner Künstler created a furore and was closed after just a few days. However, the interest and the uproar that it aroused ensured its success. In cooperation with the art dealer Eduard Schulte, many paintings from the exhibition travelled on to Cologne and Düsseldorf before returning to Berlin, where they were shown at the Equitable Palace late in the year. Munch's celebrated work *The Scream* also had its first showing at an exhibition in Berlin. It was also during this Berlin period that Munch began work in earnest on what would later become known as "The Frieze of Life", a project he returned to frequently in his remaining years.

"The Frieze of Life" is broadly concerned with love, angst and death. The series includes major individual works such as *Madonna* (1894–95), *Melancholy* (1892), *The Kiss* (1892) and *Dance of Life* (1899–1900). There are agonising representations of estrangement, as in *Ashes* (1894), motifs relating to sickness and death, such as

*The Day after,* (1894-95), oil on canvas, 115 x 152 cm. This picture was painted while Munch was staying in Berlin.

*Death in the Sick-Room* (1893), and depictions of sheer angst, such as *The Scream*, which is undoubtedly Munch's single most famous work. Elements of the landscape around Åsgårdstrand crop up repeatedly in the "Frieze of Life". From 1889 onward, Munch frequently spent the summer in this little coastal town on the western shore of Oslo Fjord. The characteristic shoreline runs like a common thread through many of his pictures, including *Dance of Life* (see p. 59) and *Melancholy* (see p. 27).

*Parisian Model,* (1896), oil on canvas, 80 x 60 cm. In 1896 Munch exhibited his works in the Salon des Indépendents in Paris for the first time.

During his stay in Berlin, Munch began working with printing techniques. His first etchings and lithographs date from the year 1894. Later he would also work with woodcuts, developing a technique of his own whereby separate expanses to be printed in different colours are cut from each other, almost like the pieces of a jigsaw puzzle, thus avoiding the need for a separate block for each of the colours to be printed. Munch's graphic oeuvre, which consists of many thousands of works, includes numerous motifs that he also explored in his paintings.

In the years from Munch's first visit to Berlin through to 1908, his life and artistic activity seem to have been hectic. He spent a lot of time away from Norway, painted a number of major works and took part in many exhibitions. His graphic output grew to large proportions. He completed a range of portraits, including one of the doctor Max Linde's children. Linde proved important to Munch in many ways, not least as a patron, while of major significance for him in Norway was the art collector Olaf Schou.

*Autumn Ploughing*, 1919, oil on canvas, 110.5 x 145.5 cm. The painting belongs to a series of motifs that Munch started painting after he bought Ekely in 1916.

In October 1908, Munch's roving, Bohemian lifestyle proved too much. Following a nervous breakdown, he became a patient of Dr. Daniel Jacobsen at his private clinic just outside Copenhagen. Even during this sojourn Munch continued to work, creating numerous drawings and prints with motifs from the zoo that lay nearby. During this period of sickness, Munch was knighted with the Royal Order of St. Olav. He also organised two major exhibitions for 1909, one of them at Blomqvist Fine Art in Kristiania (Oslo). After his convalescence at the clinic, Munch returned to Norway to take up a more reclusive and orderly way of life. There he bought the property Skrubben in Kragerø. In response to an invitation, he spent the summer of 1909 working on designs for the decoration of the main auditorium of the university in the capital. Following a complex selection procedure, Munch was ultimately granted the commission, and the paintings were completed in 1916.

In the spring of the same year Munch bought Ekely in Vestre Aker outside Kristiania (Oslo). This was a relatively large agricultural property with plentiful space for Munch's winter studio. His life at this time was considerably calmer than it had been around the turn of the century, and a range of new motifs began to appear in his pictures, many related to agriculture and working life. He also painted a series of pictures of his "best friends" – his dogs. Among the themes that preoccupied him was the cold blue nights of winter, which he combined with scenes from Henrik Ibsen's play *John Gabriel Borkman*.

During his years at Ekely Munch was highly productive, making frequent use of his printing presses for graphic works. Following the successful decoration of the university auditorium, he hoped for more commissions for public projects. But few such projects would reach fruition. On 23 January 1944, Munch died peacefully at Ekely.

Edvard Munch bequeathed both his artistic estate and his property to the city of Oslo. The bequest formed the basis for the Munch Museum, which opened in 1963, a century after the artist's birth. The National Gallery was the first public collection to acquire works by Edvard Munch, the first of them from the National Annual Autumn Exhibition of 1891. This purchase helped establish Munch's reputation at a time when his art was controversial. Several of Munch's most significant works ended up in the National Gallery, many of them donated by the art collector Olaf Schou. Schou was the source for no less than eleven of the collection's 58 paintings and water colours by Munch. In some cases Schou purchased works with the intention of handing them straight on to the National Gallery. In addition, Munch enjoyed robust support from the National Gallery's first director, Jens Thiis, who was himself responsible for a number of works finding their way into the collection. In 1933 Thiis published an extensive monograph on Munch and his art. Later he was the principal figure behind the Munch Room at the National Gallery, which was inaugurated as part of the institution's centenary celebrations in 1937.

Ellen J. Lerberg

*Night in Nice,* (1891), oil on canvas, 48 x 54 cm. This was the first painting by Edvard Munch to be acquired by the National Gallery.

# DESCRIPTIVE TEXTS

# *The Sick Child,* (1885–86)

Oil on canvas, 120 x 118.5 cm
NG.M.00839

A sickbed. The composition is simple, with the main motif placed centrally and in the foreground of the picture. Details are toned down to allow certain conspicuous elements to stand out: the girl's head against the white pillow, the bent neck of the woman and the point of contact between the two. The painting is generally regarded as Munch's breakthrough, demonstrating his turn towards a more personal and emotionally-charged form of expression. The picture is often associated with the loss of his elder sister, Sophie, who died of tuberculosis in 1877. Sick girls and dying children were, moreover, a popular subject for many of the more realistically-oriented painters of the period.

Munch himself described the picture as his farewell to realism. With its materiality and sketchy style it stands out from the more crystal-clear, true-to-life realism that dominated among Munch's contemporaries. Thickly applied layers of paint occur alongside thin, trickling stripes, pastose brushstrokes with scratch marks and surface abrasions. Attention is drawn to the picture's physical surface and its means of production. It appears sketchy and unfinished, as if the artist had halted work in the midst of the creative process. Here Munch makes an earnest bid to become master of the "unfinished" artwork.

The work was first shown at the National Annual Autumn Exhibition in 1886, although on that occasion it bore the title *Study*. The painting's unconventional aspects prompted outrage and indignation, although it also attracted a degree of approval. The scandal ensured the painting's success and its enduring position as one of the best known and most discussed of Munch's works. In due course he painted no less than six versions of the motif. Initially the National Gallery acquired a later version, thanks to a bequest from Olaf Schou in 1909. But in 1931 this was exchanged for Munch's first version of the painting from 1885–86. Schou's picture is now in the Göteborg Museum of Art.

ØU

# Self-Portrait, (1886)

Oil on canvas, 33 x 24.5 cm
NG.M.01915


In the course of his long life, Munch painted a number of self-portraits. We can follow him through many of life's vicissitudes, from a
young and decadent artist to an elderly, sick man staring death in the
face. (See p. 75.) These pictures afford us intimate insights into the
artist's life.

It is the arrogant and self-assured Bohemian we meet in this self-
portrait from 1886. The artist was 22 years old at the time and at an
early stage in his career. But despite his youthfulness, he was already
being noticed among artistic circles in his home country.

The portrait shows us the radical ways in which Munch's painting
was developing in these years. Here he has used surface scratching,
and the face seems enveloped in haze. This was a technique he also
used in his most famous painting of the 1880s, *The Sick Child* from
1885–86. Later he would change his painting style in favour of a more
flowing brushstroke.

The portrait was purchased by the National Gallery in 1938 with
funds provided by Olaf Schou. Formerly it was owned by the lawyer
Harald Nørregaard, who was married to the painter Aase Nørregaard,
a close friend of Munch.

ML

# *Hans Jæger*, 1889

Oil on canvas, 109 x 84 cm
NG.M.00485

In the 1880s Edvard Munch often found human subjects among his close family and friends. One eloquent portrait is that of the writer, anarchist and social critic Hans Jæger. The subject sits leaning back in a sofa, weighing us up through his spectacles with a direct gaze. His hat and tight-fitting overcoat emphasise his aloof and impassive aspect. The cool light streaming in through the curtains to the left casts deep shadows creating shimmers of red-violet, brown and blue-green hues. The pastose, emphatic brushstrokes seem tossed onto the canvas with the same casual attitude as the character on the sofa.

Hans Jæger was a central figure in the group known as the Christiania Bohemians – a small but conspicuous group of young students, artists and writers living in the capital who shared radical and incisively critical views on bourgeois society. Munch belonged to this circle in the 1880s. Their "credo" was partly summed up in the commandment: "Thou shalt write thy life." Jæger's book *From Christiania's Bohemia* (1885) was banned due to what were regarded at the time as pornographic scenes, for which in 1886 he was fined and sent to prison.

Although Munch gradually distanced himself from the Bohemian circle, he retained his respect for Jæger – almost ten years his senior – as both an individual and an idealist. For many years the painting remained in Munch's possession, and was shown in most of his exhibitions in the 1890s. In 1897 he offered it to the National Gallery, which duly purchased it, whereupon the Bohemian found his place on the wall alongside national literary heroes such as Bjørnstjerne Bjørnson.

FB

# *Night in Saint-Cloud*, (1890)

Oil on canvas, 64.5 x 54 cm
NG.M.01111

In the years 1889–91, Munch lived in France, supported by an artist's bursary from the Norwegian state. When cholera broke out in Paris in December 1889, Munch moved to Saint-Cloud, outside the city. There he rented the floor above a café, which commanded a beautiful view of the Seine. In the atmospheric and melancholy *Night in Saint-Cloud*, we see both the inside of his dark room and the view through the window late at night. At the window sits a man lost in thought. It might be a friend, the Danish poet Emanuel Goldstein. Shortly afterwards, Munch would design the vignette for Goldstein's anthology of symbolist poems *Alruner* (1891), an illustration that served as predecessor to *Melancholy* (1892, see p. 27), now in the National Museum's collection.

In the catalogue to his 1929 exhibition at Blomqvist Fine Art, Munch published a few "Brief excerpts from my diaries – 1889–1929". Among the various remarks, we find the famous statement that later became known as his "artistic manifesto". He dated this to Saint-Cloud 1889: "The subjects of painting will no longer be interiors, with people reading and women knitting. / They will be living, breathing people who feel and love and suffer–. / People will understand what is sacred in these things and doff their hats as in a church." This is followed by a remark which the artist dates to 1889–1900: "I paint not what I see but what I saw." In these statements Munch registers his distance from the accurate depictions of realism. *Night in Saint-Cloud* was painted at around the time he wrote this "manifesto". But it took several years before Munch seriously rejected the inner world in favour of the exterior one.

*Night in Saint-Cloud* was first exhibited at the National Annual Autumn Exhibition in 1890 with the title *Night*. It was purchased for the National Gallery from Dr. Fredrik Arentz' estate in 1917.

ML

# *Rue Lafayette*, 1891

Oil on canvas, 92 x 73 cm
NG.M.01725

In 1889, when Munch received a bursary from the Norwegian state, he went to Paris, where he familiarised himself with the period's contemporary painters. The big city and modern life. Rhythm, pulse and movement.

In the second half of the 19th century, Paris underwent major changes in its urban planning. Old buildings and districts were torn down to make way for long, broad, straight avenues and boulevards. These rapidly became part of the city's visual identity and a popular subject for many of the period's most influential artists, who were interested in depicting life in the modern metropolis.

The vantage point, the dramatic perspective and the diffuse form in this picture owe a lot to impressionist painting. The paint is applied in rhythmical, speckled and slanting strokes creating a radiant, vibrant overall effect. Here Munch has combined a punctual brushstroke with a concise style that points beyond the subject matter that is actually registered.

In spring 1891, Munch occupied rooms at Rue Lafayette no. 49. Presumably it is the view from his own rooms that he has taken as the basis for this painting. To the left we glimpse the Rue Drouot and the Rue Faubourg-Montmartre. The impression of bustling, pulsating life out on the street is offset by the sombre figure on the balcony. The painting shows Munch's strong interest in impressionism during this period. It remained, however, an interlude, and in the years that followed he preferred to explore other directions.

The picture was purchased for the National Gallery in 1933 with funds donated by Olaf Schou.

ØU

# *Melancholy,* (1892)

Oil on canvas, 64 x 96 cm
NG.M.02813

The dark shoreline curves diagonally in across the picture. On the jetty in the background we can make out three figures. The man in the foreground has turned his back on them. His head and his drooping shoulders stand out distinctly against the pale beach, a shape that is reiterated in the large boulders. The colours, primarily melancholy shades of blue, are softened by the summer night. Here we see a clear symbolist tendency in the simplification and stylisation of form and colours. In a text that can be linked to this motif, Munch noted:

> I was walking along the shore – the moon was shining through dark clouds. The stones loomed out of the water, like mysterious inhabitants of the sea. There were large, broad heads that grinned and laughed. Some of them up on the beach, others down in the water. The dark, bluish-violet sea rose and fell – sighs in among the stones … but there is life over there on the jetty. It was a man and a woman – then came another man – with oars across his shoulder. And the boat lay down there – ready to go.

The picture's thematic content refers to Munch's friend Jappe Nilssen and his unhappy love life around this time. The landscape is based on the coastline at Åsgårdstrand.

The motif exists in several versions – both as paintings and woodcuts. This too was shown in Berlin in autumn 1892, when Munch's exhibition at the Verein Berliner Künstler was forcefully criticised in the press and closed after just a few days. The controversy surrounding the exhibition served, however, to draw attention to Munch and his pictures, ensuring that they were energetically discussed in artistic circles.

The painting was a bequest from Charlotte and Christian Mustad in 1959. It was incorporated in the collection in 1970.

MY

# Inger in Black and Violet, 1892

Oil on canvas, 172.5 x 122.5 cm
NG.M.00499

In the portrait of Edvard Munch's sister Inger we see a young woman standing face on, erect and monumental. Her expression is controlled yet guarded, her posture constrained, her gaze thoughtful and introverted. Her hands are folded and her hair is tied back away from her pale face. The impression of chaste modesty is reinforced by the high black collar of her dress, tightly clasping her neck.

Inger Munch stands in front of a cool blue-grey wall that seems to form a vacuum around her, thus underlining the impression of isolation. At the same time the colour of the floor on which she is standing is warm and earthy. This surprising colour contrast creates a complex statement that alternates between the ethereal and the earthbound.

Edvard Munch is well known for the psychological depth he gives to personal characteristics. This portrait of his sister is one of his first monumental full-length portraits. Here he follows a long art historical tradition. In his portraits, Munch concentrates on the essential element of the model. He often places his figures against empty or only very sparsely furnished rooms, allowing their personality to be conveyed by their posture, eyes, face and hands, together with the expressive qualities of the colours employed.

This picture was purchased for the National Gallery in 1899.

NDN

# The Scream, 1893

Tempera and crayon on cardboard, 91 x 73.5 cm
NG.M.00939

*The Scream* is the best known and most frequently reproduced of all Munch's motifs. With its expressive colours, its flowing lines and striking overall effect, its appeal is universal.

Despite radical simplification, the landscape in the picture is recognisable as the Kristiania Fjord seen from Ekeberg, with a broad view over the fjord, the town and the hills beyond. In the background to the left, at the end of the path with the balustrade that cuts diagonally across the picture, we see two strolling figures, often regarded as two friends whom Munch mentions in notes relating to the picture. But the figure in the foreground is the first to capture the viewer's attention. Its hands are held to its head and its mouth is wide open in a silent scream, which is amplified by the undulating movement running through the surrounding landscape. The figure is ambiguous and it is hard to say whether it is a man or a woman, young or old – or even if it is human at all.

As with many of Munch's pictures, it is assumed that here as well his starting point was private feelings and experience. His diaries contain several remarks that seem to form a background to this depiction of existential angst, among them the following: "I was walking along the road with two friends – Then the sun went down – The sky suddenly turned to blood and I felt a great scream in nature –".

*The Scream* was first exhibited at Munch's solo exhibition in Berlin in 1893. It was a central element in "The Frieze of Life", and has been the theme of probing analysis and many suggested interpretations. The painting also exists in a later version, which is in the possession of the Munch Museum. In addition Munch worked with the motif in drawings, pastels and prints.

The National Museum's picture was donated to the museum by Olaf Schou in 1910.

MY

# Moonlight, (1893)

Oil on canvas, 140.5 x 137 cm
NG.M.01914

A finely tuned interplay of contrasts is one of the defining features of this evocative painting. Intense, cool moonlight falls on a picket fence and a window frame behind the woman in the foreground, while also illuminating her pale face. The rest of the woman's figure, together with the shadow on the wall and the garden, lies in muffled obscurity. Here we find shapes with concise, undulating contours that stand in contrast with the rhythmically patterned, rectangular forms of the fence and the house. Set against these flat, frontal elements, the woman's shadow and the sections of fence and wall create an element of depth in the composition. But the visual components are not in themselves what matter most; the concise, underlying mood is one of loneliness, yearning and angst.

Munch painted this picture in summer 1893 at Åsgårdstrand, where he also painted *The Voice* (now in the Munch Museum), which tackles a related theme. Three years later he returned to this motif in a woodcut (cf. p. 49).

The painting was purchased for the National Gallery in 1938 with funds donated by Olaf Schou, with a contribution from Marit Nørregaard.

SH

# Death in the Sick-Room (prob. 1893)

Tempera and crayon on canvas, 152.5 x 169.5 cm
NG.M.00940

The picture shows what we can assume to be the artist's family grouped around his sister Sophie, who died in 1877. She is sitting in a chair with her back to us. To the right stands an aunt, Karen Bjølstad, who moved in with the family to take care of the children and the household after the mother died of tuberculosis in 1868. In the background stands the father, the doctor Christian Munch, with his hands clasped as if in prayer. Near the centre of the picture is a male figure, probably Edvard, in quarter-face. Sister Laura is sitting in the foreground with her hands in her lap, while the third sister, Inger, stands staring straight at us. The male figure to the left is generally identified as Edvard's younger brother Andreas. In *Death in the Sick-Room* there is no physical contact between the people, except for the hand that aunt Karen has laid on the back of the chair in which the invalid sits.

The subject of sickness was so widespread in the late 1800s that those years have been called the "pillow period" in Scandinavian painting. "Sickness, madness and death were the black angels who watched over my cradle," Munch wrote.

"I paint not what I see, but what I saw," Munch once said about his works. This is a situation recalled from several years earlier, to which he returned in the 1890s. The scene is strictly composed, and excludes anything irrelevant to the theme. The dark clothes and the noxious green of the bedroom walls intensify the mood of discomfort.

The painting was given to the National Gallery by Olaf Schou in 1910.

EH

# *Ashes*, (1894)

Oil on canvas, 120.5 x 141 cm
NG.M.00809


Against a dark background of slender tree trunks, a woman in pale clothing stands facing us. Her wide eyes, loose hair and open bodice tell us of what has happened. With her hands high on her head, her posture is expressive of despair, but also of power and victory. In the lower left quarter of the picture sits a man with his back turned to the woman. He is withdrawn and holds his hands dejectedly to his head. The only contact between the two after what has just happened in the sombre woods is through her long, red hair.

"I felt our love lying on the earth like a heap of ash," Munch wrote on a lithographic version of the motif. This explains both the picture's title and the stylised tree trunk in front of the man. Also in its use of colour and form, this picture is full of contrasts and tension: open and closed shapes, straight and curved lines, dark and light colours.

This painting is possibly one of Munch's most pessimistic on the subject of male – female relationships. It depicts the man as weak and the loser, while the woman is strong and victorious. In this work Munch expresses both personal experience and typical aspects of the complex contemporary view of woman: "The woman who is at one and the same time a saint – a whore – and unhappily devoted."

The painting was purchased for the museum in 1909.

FB

# Madonna, (1894–95)

Oil on canvas, 90.5 x 70.5 cm
NG.M.00841

One of the most important and best known motifs of Munch's oeuvre, *Madonna* was at the centre of his "Frieze of Life" series. The motif exists in several versions and originally bore the title *Kvinne som elsker* (Woman making Love). The painting was first displayed in a frame decorated with sperm cells and a foetus.

We are shown a woman whose half-closed eyes and posture seem to indicate love-making and the fateful moment of conception. Softly undulating lines form a kind of cyclical form around her reminiscent of an aura. Above her head hangs a "halo" – not golden, but red, like passion, pain and life. Both the halo and the picture's title are religious allusions that form a surprising contrast to the motif's evidently erotic aspect. At the same time, these religious elements emphasise the existential seriousness of the picture's theme.

Concerning this motif, Munch himself said:

> The pause when the entire world stopped in its tracks. Your face encompasses all the beauty of the earthly realm. Your lips, crimson red like the coming fruit, drift apart as if in pain. The smile of a corpse – Now life reaches out a hand to death. The link is forged that binds a thousand generations past to a thousand generations to come.

The painting was a gift from Olav Schou in 1909.

NDN

# *Puberty*, (1894–95)

Oil on canvas, 151.5 x 110 cm
NG.M.00807

A naked young girl with loose hair is sitting on the edge of a bed, hiding her crotch with her arms. She stares at us with wide-open eyes. The composition is simple, with the frontally depicted body vertical in contrast to the horizontal lines of the bed. To the left of the girl lies a pillow, to the right a large, dark shadow is thrown on the lighter wall.

The National Museum's version of this motif was painted in Berlin in the winter of 1894–95. Aspects of *Puberty* link it to the naturalism of the 1880s. The girl's skinny arms and immature breasts combined with her relatively large hands and feet are realistically rendered. At the same time the painting has elements that anticipate Munch's later, more expressive style. The picture deals with a girl's approach to sexual maturity in a manner that is frank and unembellished. The threatening shadow can be seen as a projection of the girl's inner state of mind. Comparable shadows feature in several other works by Munch.

Many people have wondered how a male artist could empathise with the emotional world of a young girl in this way. A verbal counterpart of this mood is provided by the Polish poet Stanislav Przybyszewski, who was closely attached to the Scandinavian circle in Berlin at the time:

> She sensed it, she didn't understand [...] She couldn't imagine, she merely felt the wild, quivering shudder surge through her body. She clasped both her hands between her knees, bent forwards and pulled in her feet, and there she sat, huddled up on the edge of the bed, listening in anxious pain to something unfamiliar and frightening. What was it? It came so often, always afresh! It frightened her. It made her tremble. The entire house was full of ghosts.
> (Translated from *Underveis*, Kra: 1895).

The picture was purchased in 1909 with a donation from the A.C. Houen Fund.

EH

# Self-Portrait with Cigarette, 1895

Oil on canvas, 110.5 x 85.5 cm
NG.M.00470


Edvard Munch has depicted himself with his face turned to the viewer. The artist's face and hands are conspicuously emphasised and seem almost luminous against the dark, unarticulated background. For an artist, these parts of the body are especially significant. At the centre of the composition, one hand is raised to chest height, as if held to the heart. Although the artist seems to be gazing intensely at the viewer, he is looking no less into himself and his world. The artist is illuminated from below and together with the diffuse background and the smoke from the cigarette, this lends the picture a hint of mystery.

Munch was 31 when he painted this picture. A few years earlier he had been part of the circle that met at the café-bar "Zum schwarzen Ferkel" in Berlin. One central member of this group was August Strindberg, although no less important to Munch were the Polish poet and pianist Stanislaw Przybyszewski and his wife Dagny Juel. Przybyszewski contributed to the first monograph about Munch. Strindberg's interest in mysticism and the occult and his thoughts about his own paintings may have been significant to Munch. Strindberg regarded himself as a medium, link, or conduit for what was captured on the canvas.

The painting was purchased from the artist in 1895.

EL

# *Moonlight*, 1895

Oil on canvas, 93 x 110 cm
NG.M.02815

This painting shows one of Munch's most simplified depictions of
the Norwegian coastal landscape in the light of a summer night.
Thematically it is related to *The Voice*, which Munch had painted
earlier, in that case with a female figure in the central foreground.
*Moonlight* captures a mood of nature, without human presence. The
first thing to catch our attention is the unusual pillar of moonlight,
a motif that occurs in several of Munch's pictures. The next is the
undulating coastline, which forms a horizontal counterpoint to the
strict verticality of the trees. The colours are subdued, but there are
clear contrasts between the dark forest floor, the white shore and the
intense blue of the water. Details are simplified and subordinated to
the overall scheme, but without compromising the landscape's characteristic features and recognisability. Instead of depicting an action,
the picture expresses a certain mood. At the same time there is a
formal theme in the pillar of moonlight, the strict verticality of the
trees, the gentle curves of the shoreline, and the water as a symbol of
the masculine and the feminine.

The motif probably derived from the area around Åsgårdstrand,
where Munch stayed this summer. It was a place to which he was
very attached. The sea and the landscape both attracted and inspired
him, and elements of nature in the region appear in a range of pictures from the 1890s. Running through these images, Munch wrote,
"twists the flowing shoreline, beyond lies the sea, which is always in
motion, and beneath the canopy of trees varied life unfolds with its
joys and cares."

The painting was a bequest from Charlotte and Christian Mustad in
1959. It was incorporated in the collection in 1970.

MY

# Young Woman washing herself, (1896)

Oil on panel, 74.5 x 59 cm
NG.M.00843

A young woman stands washing herself. The room is simple and austere. There is no indication of opulence or a luxurious way of life. Half turned away, the girl's naked back and slender figure is illuminated by light from the window in the background. The window seems to echo the picture's upright format, marking a separation from the world outside. Is it sunlight or moonlight that we see, morning or evening, day or night?

The scene is intimate and revealing. We are witness to a private moment in which the woman is also vulnerable. Such intimate interior scenes were popular in the late 19th century, especially in Paris, where artists such as Edgar Degas, Henri de Toulouse-Lautrec and Pierre Bonnard worked with this kind of motif. Munch painted the picture during a stay in Paris in 1896. For several years he had been depicting women in various large format, broodingly symbolic works linked to his "Frieze of Life" (including *Madonna*, *The Kiss*, *Vampire* and *Dance of Life*). In this work the woman is depicted in a more prosaic and mundane context. It is one of the first in a series of related nude studies that shows a different aspect of Munch's creative activity.

The paint is applied in thin, semi-transparent layers, creating an almost translucent quality. The texture of the wood panel on which the work is painted can be seen in many parts of the picture. Together with the subtle use of colour, this creates a poetic dimension, while simultaneously emphasising the work's inherent pictorial quality.

This painting was donated to the National Gallery by Olaf Schou in 1909.

ØU

# Moonlight, (1896)

Coloured woodcut, 410 x 465 mm
NG.K&H.B.00615, (GW 90)

*Moonlight* was one of Munch's first coloured woodcuts. It was created in Paris in 1896. Munch began working with prints in Berlin in the autumn of 1894, initially with etchings, and after a short time, with lithographs, in both cases in black and white. But the use of colour intrigued him. In Paris he collaborated with the renowned printer Auguste Clot, together with whom he created, among other things, the lithograph *The Sick Child*, both in black and white and a range of colour versions. In parallel, Munch began working with woodcuts. From that point on he was not just a masterly exponent of graphic techniques, he also became a significant pioneer in the field.

For *Moonlight* Munch used several blocks. But rather than create a single block for each colour in the print, he cut up a single block, inking each of the pieces separately and then putting the pieces back together again (the puzzle method). He varied the colours he used in a range of prints, frequently reworking and printing from the same blocks at later times. For example, he produced a new version of *Moonlight* in 1902. The National Museum's print however apparently belongs to those created in 1896. Characteristic of Munch's woodcuts, in addition to the puzzle method, is the simplification of the formal language, the rough cuts in the blocks and the use of the woodgrain to create a surface pattern in the print. His characteristic style became influential for later generations of woodcut artists.

The motif of this print is a (mirror inverted) section of the painting *Moonlight* from 1893 (p. 33). Munch regarded repetitions of this kind as new versions. Smaller or larger differences in the cropping of the motif, form, colour and materiality added nuances to the visual statement.

It is not known when the National Gallery acquired the woodcut *Moonlight*.

SH

# Separation II, 1896

Lithograph printed in blue, 410 x 610 mm
NG.K&H.A.19030, (GW 78)

The blue used to print this lithograph reinforces the melancholy mood of the subject. With his eyes closed and his head bowed, the pale-faced man appears introverted and passive. The woman, who has turned away from him and is looking out to sea, is in the process of leaving the man, while the wind blows her long hair back towards his chest. In contrast to the darkness of the man, the woman is paler. The contrast between them is further emphasised by the drawing technique, the emphatic and energetic use of the lithographic tool in the depiction of the man, while a looser and more sensitive line is used for the female profile.

The motif may be interpreted as related to a separation experienced by the artist himself, and alluded to in his notes: "But even once she has vanished across the sea he feels / That delicate single threads are stuck fast in his heart / – it bleeds – and smarts like an eternally open wound."

*Separation II* exists as a single-colour print, both with and without colouring, but also as a multi-coloured print. There are two lithographic versions of the separation motif – both from 1896. The version we have here concentrates on the heads of the couple. The motif is also rendered in a painting from 1893 and in another from 1896. In addition there are several sketches with related motifs from the years 1895 and 1896.

It is unclear when the National Gallery acquired this lithograph.

MT

# Two Human Beings (The Lonely Ones), 1896

Drypoint, 150 x 217 mm
NG.K&H.A.19063, (GW 13)

The title *Two Human Beings* is a straightforward description of the motif of this graphic print; *The Lonely Ones* describes the picture's mood. Two figures with their backs to the viewer – a woman and a man – dominate the composition. The distance between them, the contrast between his dark and her light figure and the subtle twist in the man's torso towards the woman express both attraction and distance. The shore on which they stand and the water they are facing emphasise the mood of yearning and loneliness both thematically and visually. This black and white print is executed in drypoint, a technique which allows soft strokes and surface effects. Munch's finely tuned use of this technique and of half-tone, ranging from dazzling white through to fuzzy darkness, together with the intimate format and tight cropping of the subject, all enhance the tense calm of this love motif.

Munch began working with printmaking in Berlin in autumn 1894 and the plates for *Two Human Beings* are among the first he created. This print is one of eight that made up a portfolio published by the art historian Julius Meier-Graefe in 1895. The National Museum's copy is dated 1896. Whether or not it is in fact attributable to that year is unclear. Nevertheless, this expressive little print strikingly illustrates that Munch was a masterly graphic artist from the very outset. The print reiterates (in mirror image) the motif of a painting Munch had worked on in the 1890s. That painting has since been lost, although we know of it from a photograph. Munch repeated the motif later in coloured woodcuts (1899 and 1917).

It is unclear when the museum acquired *Two Human Beings*, but it could have been as early as 1898.

SH

# *Encounter in Space* (1898–99)

Coloured woodcut, 190 x 252 mm
NG.K&H.A.19103, (GW 136)

Two people – a woman and a man – float toward one another in apparent weightlessness against a dark background. Contours of sperm cells surround the couple. The erotic tension is the dominant element of this motif. The two people seem attracted to one another by subconscious powers. The contrast between the couple's physical proximity and a certain emotive distance is suggested by the averted faces. In one of his commentaries on this picture, Munch compared people's lives with the planets: "Human fates are like planets. They appear from the unknown only to meet and disappear." This reference to a cosmic dimension is also reflected in the title of the woodcut.

The National Museum's woodcut is printed in black, red and turquoise. In some variants of the motif turquoise is replaced with blue or yellowish green. The red figure of the man suggests pain and passion towards the woman, whereas her own bluish-green colour shows a cooler attitude in contrast. At the same time, the woman has turned to face empty space, whereas the inward curve of the man's head and back are more introverted. This woodcut was printed from a single block of wood sawn into three pieces – the so-called puzzle method. Two small fragments have been replaced near the feet of the man and the woman, following damage to the block.

Among Munch's graphic works we find a related motif in the lithograph *Decorative Sketch* from 1897/98, and in 1902 Munch returned to the subject in etching.

It is uncertain when the National Gallery acquired this work.

MT

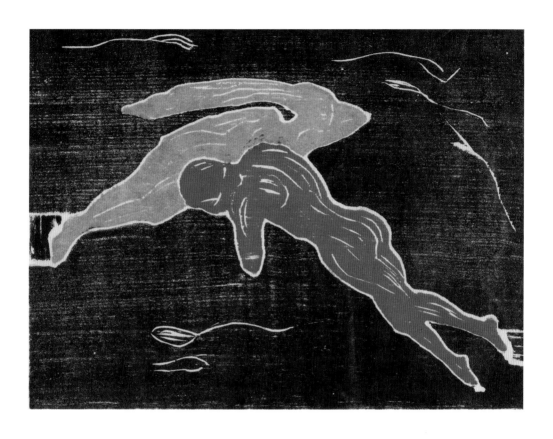

# *Winter,* (1899)

Oil on cardboard, 60.5 x 90 cm
NG.M.00570

Landscape was an important genre for Munch. In the years around the turn of the century, he created a number of landscapes with winter motifs from Nordstrand just outside the capital. In the painting *Winter* we find ourselves gazing into a dark spruce forest illuminated by light reflected from the snow-covered earth. Although there are no people here, we see traces in the snow, where some lonely traveller has passed along the path in the foreground. The mood is heavy with silence and meditative calm.

The picture is sketchily painted. We see how the brush has swept over the snow-covered trees in quick, gentle arcs. In many places the underlying brown cardboard is visible through the thin layer of oil paint. The picture's fine balance between straight and curved lines, dark and light areas, between flat expanses and perspective effects is typical of Munch's landscape art. Through the simplification of form and the play of line he draws attention to the picture surface. At the same time, the sloping line of the path, the rapidly diminishing height of the trees and the subtle light effects all establish the forest as a space.

Like many Scandinavian artists around this period, Munch was interested in what was generally referred to as the landscape of the mind. "Nature is not visible only to the eye. It is also the soul's inner pictures – pictures on the back of the eye," as Munch himself put it. The artist is rooted in a concrete landscape, while at the same time emphasising the subjective experience of nature's mystical aspect through his personal use of composition, light, colour and form.

The painting was purchased for the National Gallery in 1901.

FB

# Dance of Life, 1899–1900

Oil on canvas, 125 x 191 cm
NG.M.00941

Munch's painting shows several couples dancing in a luminous summer night. The central element of the composition is a couple, of whom the woman is wearing a bright red dress that wraps itself around the feet of her dancing partner. Her loose hair swirling about him, they seem to become a single entity. This couple is flanked by two other women, one of them young and radiant in a white dress, the other pale, with sunken cheeks and dressed in black. It is as if a story were being told about various stages in a woman's life. Munch has set the scene on the seashore, a landscape with elements from Åsgårdstrand. Many of the pictures in Munch's protracted "Frieze of Life" project were inspired by Åsgårdstrand's curving shoreline and characteristic landscape.

In 1898 Munch received a copy of Helge Rode's new theatre play *Dansen gaar* (The Dance Goes On). Rode's play may well have inspired Munch's motif. In the play, the artist Aage Vollmer says:

> The dance of life. My picture shall be called The Dance of Life! There will be a couple dancing in flowing garments [...] He is holding her tight. He is profoundly serious and happy. [...] He will hold her so close, so tight, that she almost merges with him. [...] He infuses her with strength.

Munch kept Helge Rode's play in his library, although it was not his only inspiration for this picture. The motif probably also reflects personal experience. *Dance of Life* was a key work in the "Frieze of Life".

The painting was bought by Olaf Schou at the Munch exhibition at the Diorama hall in Kristiania in 1910 and immediately presented to the National Gallery.

EL

# *The Girls on the Bridge*, (1901)

Oil on canvas, 136 x 125 cm
NG.M.00844

This painting indicates a new departure in Munch's art. It was created shortly after the turn of the century after Munch had absorbed
impressions of monumental renaissance art during a journey to Italy.
The image of the three girls leaning over the balustrade, the mansion
with the large tree and the full moon in the bright summer night is
laden with mystery.

In 1897, having bought a little house at Åsgårdstrand, Munch remar-
ked: "To walk around here is like walking among my pictures. I feel
such an urge to paint when walking around in Åsgårdstrand". The
shoreline with its many bays and treetops reflected in the water are
familiar from other landscape paintings. The undulating rhythm of
the lines is comparable to the art nouveau style. The diagonal of the
balustrade is reminiscent of *The Scream*, although here the sloping
perspective lines are intercepted by the horizontal white garden wall.

The artist summarises his complete visual impression in a simplified
composition in which nature, buildings and the figures interact to
create an atmosphere of contemplation. His palette is brighter and
fresher than in the pictures of the 1890s. Together with the beige-
pink of the road and the bridge, the subdued green and blue tones
help to create the lyrical nocturnal mood, which is enhanced by the
pale yellow moon. The white, red and green dresses of the young girls
boldly accentuate the use of colour. There exist many versions of this
picture, which was one of Munch's most popular motifs.

The painting was donated to the museum by Olaf Schou in 1909.

EH

# The Kiss IV, (1902)

Two-colour woodcut, 471 x 476 mm
NG.K&H.A.19517, (GW 204)


The kissing couple is monumentally placed at the centre of the picture. The figures are considerably simplified and almost merge with one another. The motif expresses harmony, empathy and warmth.

The woodcut has been printed in black and a delicate grey-green tone from two blocks – a figure block that has been worked with gouges and a fretsaw, and a seemingly unworked background block with a vertical grain pattern. Munch was very interested in the visual effect of woodgrain and the textures it produced. In addition to being decorative elements, woodgrain and branch knots added life and movement to the picture.

There are four variations of the woodcut on this theme. *The Kiss I* and *II* were produced in 1897 and were among Munch's earliest woodcuts. *The Kiss III* was created in 1898 and *The Kiss IV* in 1902. In each case the artist varies the nuances of the background by using different blocks that have been somewhat modified.

Munch painted this motif several times between 1892 and 1897. The version in the National Museum dates from 1892. The subject was first executed in print in an etching from 1895. Munch frequently returned to his previous motifs in order to explore them in other media. The characteristics of the various media enabled him to seek new expressive possibilities.

We do not know when the National Gallery acquired *The Kiss IV*.

MT

# Vampire II, 1902

Lithograph and coloured woodcut, 385 x 553 mm
NG.K&H.A.18996, (GW 41)


Munch frequently repeated motifs that he found particularly inte-
resting, some of them many times and in a range of media. He first
worked with the motif seen in this print in paint in 1893. In 1896 he
produced a black and white lithograph on the theme, and in 1902
he combined lithography and woodcut. Later he painted several new
versions. The depiction of a red-haired woman leaning over the neck
of a man kneeling in front of her has clearly erotic overtones. Is she
kissing or biting him? The title *Vampire* can be traced back to the
Polish author Stanislav Przybyszewski, one of the central figures in
the circle Munch frequented in Berlin in the 1890s. It emphasises the
threatening role of the woman and the painful aspect of the man's
experience of love. Not only was this a theme that interested the Berlin circle and the Christiania Bohemians, it also preoccupied Munch
on account of personal experience. The picture has also been known
under the title *Love and Pain*.

Munch was interested in the many variations that could be achieved
through the manipulation of printing techniques. For this reason he
often used different colours in making prints from the same block,
often in unusual combinations. *Vampire II* is a fascinating example.
Here he has combined a black and white print from a lithographic
stone he had used in 1896 with coloured prints from a woodcut created in 1902. On past occasions he had cut the wood block into pieces,
applied ink to each piece individually, then reassembled them (like
a puzzle) before running off a print. There are several versions of
*Vampire II* using different colours.

We do not know when the National Gallery acquired this print.

SH

# The Fairytale Forest, (1901–02)

Oil on canvas, 79 x 106.5 cm
NG.M.02237

Six children stand with their backs to us looking towards a dense green forest. Wearing costumes typical of the period, they hold each other by the hand. They are still at a safe distance from the wood. But although it is the middle of the day, and there are no dark shadows to pose an immediate threat, it is hard to say what the forest might conceal. The path ahead disappears among the trees – do they dare to follow it? The children are the link between the viewer and the mystical forest, while at the same time serving an important compositional function in the painting.

In 1903 Dr. Max Linde asked Munch to decorate the children's room at his family villa in Lübeck, Germany. The proposals that Munch presented in December 1904 were, however, not well received. The doctor found the motifs with their kissing and dancing couples a touch too "adult" to grace a children's room. One exception may well have been *The Fairytale Forest*, although not even this was purchased by Linde. Thus the paintings for the "Linde Frieze" ended up in different places. Munch had worked on the material for *The Fairytale Forest* for some years. He took the theme further in the so-called "Freia Frieze", which was commissioned by Johan Throne Holst, director of the Freia chocolate factory for the company's 25th anniversary in 1923.

*The Fairytale Forest* was bequeathed to the museum by Alfred Larsen in 1950.

EL

# The Brooch. Eva Mudocci, 1903

Lithograph, 605 x 474 mm
NG.K&H.B.00816, (GW 244)

One of Munch's most beautiful and highly praised female figures. Eva Mudocci (Rose Lynton, prob. 1883–1953) was a young, gifted violinist whom Munch got to know in 1902. Together with the pianist Bella Edwards, she toured Europe giving concerts that brought her renown and acclaim. In the lithograph, Mudocci is depicted half-length and from a low angle. Her loose dark hair flows freely around her pale face. Her gaze is lowered and turned to one side, towards something beyond the frame and invisible to the viewer. Focal to the picture is her brooch, which creates a fine balance in the composition and enhances her enigmatic gaze. What does it mean to her? What is she thinking about? Mudocci appears in two other works Munch finished in the same year: *Violin Concert* and *Salome*.

There are certain similarities between the figure in *The Brooch* and Munch's famous *Madonna*. Earlier, this lithograph itself bore that title. Here the erotic dimension is considerably toned down and the figure shows more individual and thoughtful traits. The work demonstrates how Munch was gradually mastering the expressive potential of the lithographic medium. The undulating lines have a lot in common with the leisurely brushstrokes that characterise so many of Munch's paintings. With its simple contrasts and subtle visual effects this is a highlight among Munch's graphic works.

The work was bequeathed to the National Gallery by Hans Aas in 1947.

ØU

# Man in the Cabbage-Field, 1916

Oil on canvas, 136 x 180 cm
NG.M.01865

With its lush colours and monumental grandeur, this depiction of a farmer harvesting his produce and of the fundamental needs of life has acquired central significance among the works of Munch's later period.

After many years without a fixed abode in Europe, Munch returned to settle permanently in his native country in 1909. In 1916 he bought the rural property Ekely just outside Kristiania (Oslo), where he lived until his death in 1944. The house had a large garden that had formerly been used as an agricultural nursery. The verdant surroundings with farmers at work, horses and fields quickly spawned a series of motifs that were crucial to Munch's work in this period.

The simple composition of this picture, its light colours and rough brushstrokes have a lot in common with Munch's paintings for the university auditorium in Kristiania. The man is depicted face on, inscribed in a triangle of incisive visual force. His individual characteristics are toned down to the benefit of more general aspects.

The work was painted at a time when World War I was ravaging Europe (as a neutral country, Norway remained outside the conflict). It was a war that provided a powerful corrective to the 19th century zeal for industrial development, making it important to secure supplies of agricultural products. Munch's interest in the rural way of life in these years can be seen in connection with this history. At the same time, there are similarities between Munch's paintings of farming life and his depictions of industrial labourers, a field of interest that can be traced back to the years 1907–08.

The picture was donated to the National Gallery in 1937 by Charlotte and Christian Mustad.

ØU

# *Bathing Man,* (1918)

Oil on canvas, 160 x 110 cm
NG.M.01699

Bathers were a popular subject around the turn of the last century. Sojourns at health spas were fashionable and people pursued sports, nudism and the healthful effects of the natural environment. It was seen as cleansing to bathe in the sea, while the sun constituted a rejuvenating force of life.

In this painting we see a virile, muscular, naked man emerging from the cool, turquoise sea after a swim. The picture can be read as a reflection of the period's "vitalism" – a world view that assumed all living things to be suffused with a magical life force. This philosophy found its pictorial expression in particular in dynamic motifs of naked men and youths.

As a cultural phenomenon, vitalism was a reaction against the decadence of the period, and against industrialism, with the great cities and ways of life it brought with it. Instead of cool-headed rationalism and scientific technology, vitalism preferred to emphasise instinct and intuition – and believed the key to a better life lay in nature and good health.

The picture was a gift from the artist to the National Gallery in 1927.

NDN

# Self-Portrait with the Spanish Flu, 1919

Oil on canvas, 150 x 131 cm
NG.M.01867

Munch became ill at the turn of the year 1918–19, having apparently contracted the Spanish flu, which became a serious worldwide epidemic, taking the lives of many millions of people in the years 1917–20. In a series of studies, sketches and paintings, Munch followed the various stages of the illness, illustrating how close death came to life.

It is a sick and enfeebled artist who meets our gaze in *Self-Portrait with the Spanish Flu*. With thinning hair and sallow complexion, he is heavily wrapped in a dressing gown and blanket. Sitting in a wicker chair in front of his unmade sickbed, he shows us his frail condition. Intimate and straight to the point. The technical approach also seems direct and unembellished. The figure is depicted using simple, wavy lines and colours applied with rough sweeps of the brush. Red, blue, yellow – green and brown. The experience is concentrated in this picture. The room seems narrow and the dominant use of yellow intensifies the restlessness that characterises the composition.

The picture belongs to a late phase of Munch's art, created just a few years after he settled at Ekely on the outskirts of Kristiania (Oslo). He had recently completed the large-scale decoration of the main auditorium at the university, a work that seems to find a continuation in the colours and monumentality of this painting. Here, however, he has returned to one of his recurrent preoccupations: himself. The picture's large format, its broad painterly register and expressive force give it a unique place among Munch's many self-portraits.

The painting was donated to the National Gallery by Charlotte and Christian Mustad in 1937.

ØU

# Biography Edvard Munch

**1863**
Born 12th December at Engelhaug Farm, Løten in Hedmark.

**1881**
Enters the Royal School of Art and Design, Kristiania (now Oslo).

**1882**
Christian Krohg is Munch's tutor for a short period.

**1883**
Makes his exhibition debut at the Industry and Art Exhibition in Kristiania, showing *Study Head*.

**1884**
Awarded his first bursary, Schäffer's Legacy.

**1885**
Takes part in the World Exhibition in Antwerp. Travels to Paris for the first time.

**1886**
Takes part in the National Annual Autumn Exhibition in Kristiania with four paintings, including *The Sick Child* (1885–86).

**1889**
Mounts his first solo exhibition at the Student Association in Kristiania. Returns to Paris, where he studies for a brief period under Léon Bonnat.

**1891**
The National Gallery buys its first painting by Munch, *Night in Nice* (1891).

**1892**
Solo exhibition at Tostrupgården in Kristiania. He is invited to mount a solo exhibition at Verein Berliner Künstler. The Berlin exhibition sparks controversy and is closed after five days.

Portrait photo of Edvard Munch, 1886.
Photo: Leverin, Christiania.

**1893**
Moves to Berlin and becomes part of the circle around August Strindberg.

**1894**
Starts working with graphic prints. The first biography of the artist is published, written by Stanislav Przybyszewski, Franz Servaes, Willy Pastor and Julius Meier-Graefe.

**1896**
Exhibits for the first time at Salon des Indépendants in Paris.

**1897**
Buys a house at Åsgårdstrand, where he has spent several summers since 1889.

**1902**
Shows a series of pictures that later become known as the "Frieze of Life" at the Berliner Secession.

**1904**
Shows 20 paintings in a special "hall of honour" at the Vienna Secession.

**1905**
A highly successful exhibition in Prague.

**1908**
Admitted to Dr. Daniel Jacobsen's clinic in Copenhagen following a nervous breakdown. Awarded the Royal Order of St. Olav.

**1909**
Works on designs for the decoration of the new auditorium at the university in Kristiania.

**1912**
Contributes 32 pictures to the Sonderbund exhibition in Cologne.

**1916**
Buys the Ekely property outside Kristiania (Oslo). Completes the decoration of the university auditorium.

**1918**
Shows the "Frieze of Life" at Blomqvist Fine Art in Kristiania, at the same time publishing a leaflet with the same title in which he presents his thoughts on the project in written form.

**1922**
Paints decorations for the canteen at the Freia chocolate factory, Kristiania. These are finished in the following year.

*Self-Portrait*, 1905, water colour and pastel on cardboard, 44 x 41.5 cm.

**1927**
Major retrospective exhibition at Berlin's National Gallery. The same selection is later shown at the National Gallery, Oslo.

**1937**
Inauguration of the "Munch Room" at the National Gallery on 29th April. In Germany Munch's art is condemned as "entartet", with German museums ridding themselves of 82 of his works.

**1944**
Munch dies in his home at Ekely on 23rd January. He bequeaths his artistic estate and property to Oslo city. The bequest forms the basis for the Munch Museum, which opens in 1963.

# Illustrations

*Andreas Reading*, (1883)
Oil on cardboard, 51.5 x 35.5 cm
Signed top right: E. Munch
NG.M.02810. Bequeathed by Charlotte and
Christian Mustad in 1959, incorporated in the
collection in 1970
(Ill. page 8)

*The Sick Child*, (1885–86)
Oil on canvas, 120 x 118.5 cm
Signed lower right: E Munch
NG.M.00839. Through a bequest from Olaf
Schou in 1909 the museum acquired a later ver-
sion of the painting. In 1931 this was exchan-
ged for Munch's first version from 1885–86.
(Ill. page 17)

*Self-Portrait,* (1886)
Oil on canvas, 33 x 24.5 cm
Signed lower right: E. Munch
NG.M.01915. Bought in 1938
(Ill. page 19)

*Study for a Portrait*, 1887
Oil on canvas, 25.5 x 29 cm
Signed lower right: E.M. 87 (visible only
through x-ray)
NG.M.03054. Gift from Olaf Schou in 1909
(Ill. page 9)

*Hans Jæger*, 1889
Oil on canvas, 109 x 84 cm
Signed lower left: E Munch 1889
NG.M.00485. Bought in 1897
(Ill. page 21)

*Night in Saint-Cloud*, (1890)
Oil on canvas, 64.5 x 54 cm
Signed lower right: E Munch
NG.M.01111. Bought in 1917
(Ill. page 23)

*Rue Lafayette*, 1891
Oil on canvas, 92 x 73 cm
Signed lower right: E. Munch 91
NG.M.01725. Bought in 1933
(Ill. page 25)

*Night in Nice*, (1891)
Oil on canvas, 48 x 54 cm
Unsigned
NG.M.00394. Bought in 1891
(Ill. page 14)

*Melancholy*, (1892)
Oil on canvas, 64 x 96 cm
Signed lower left: E.M.
NG.M.02813. Bequeathed by Charlotte and
Christian Mustad in 1959, incorporated in the
collection in 1970
(Ill. page 27)

*Inger in Black and Violet*, 1892
Oil on canvas, 172.5 x 122.5 cm
Signed lower left: E. Munch 1892
NG.M.00499. Bought in 1899
(Ill. page 29)

*The Scream*, 1893
Tempera and crayon on cardboard, 91 x 73.5 cm
Signed lower left: E. Munch 1893
NG.M.00939. Gift from Olaf Schou in 1910
(Ill. page 31)

*Moonlight,* (1893)
Oil on canvas, 140.5 x 137 cm
Signed lower right: E. Munch
NG.M.01914. Bought in 1938
(Ill. page 33)

*Death in the Sick-Room,* (prob. 1893)
Tempera and crayon on canvas,
152.5 x 169.5 cm
Signed lower left: E. Munch.
NG.M.00940. Gift from Olaf Schou i 1910
(Ill. page 35)

*Ashes*, (1894)
Oil on canvas, 120.5 x 141 cm
Signed top right: E. Munch
NG.M. 00809. Bought in 1909
(Ill. page 37)

*The Day after*, (1894–95)
Oil on canvas, 115 x 152 cm
Signed lower left: E. Munch
NG.M.00808. Bought in 1909
(Ill. page 10)

*Madonna*, (1894–95)
Oil on canvas, 90.5 x 70.5 cm
Signed lower left: E Munch
NG.M.00841. Gift from Olaf Schou in 1909
(Ill. page 39)

*Puberty,* (1894–95)
Oil on canvas, 151.5 x 110 cm
Signed lower right: E. Munch
NG.M.00807. Bought in 1909
(Ill. page 41)

*Self-Portrait*, 1895
(GW 37)
Litograph, 457 x 323 mm
NG.K&H.A.18994
(Ill. page 6)

*Self-Portrait with Cigarette,* 1895
Oil on canvas, 110.5 x 85.5 cm
Signed lower left: E. Munch 1895
NG.M.00470. Bought in 1895
(Ill. page 43)

*Moonlight,* 1895
Oil on canvas, 93 x 110 cm
Signed lower left: E Munch 95
NG.M.02815. Bequeathed by Charlotte and
Christian Mustad in 1959, incorporated in the
collection in 1970
(Ill. page 45)

*Parisian Model,* (1896)
Oil on canvas, 80 x 60 cm
Signed top left: E. Munch, lower left: E.M.
NG.M.02816. Bequeathed by Charlotte and
Christian Mustad in 1959, incorporated in the
collection in 1970
(Ill. page 11)

*Young Woman washing herself,* (1896)
Oil on panel, 74.5 x 59 cm
Unsigned
NG.M.00843. Gift from Olaf Schou in 1909
(Ill. page 47)

*Moonlight,* (1896)
(GW 90)
Coloured woodcut, 410 x 465 mm
NG.K&H.B.00615
(Ill. page 49)

*Separation II*, 1896
(GW 78)
Litograph printed in blue, 410 x 610 mm
NG.K&H.A.19030
(Ill. page 51)

*Two Human Beings (The Lonely Ones)*, 1896
(GW 13)
Drypoint, 150 x 217 mm
NG.K&H.A.19063
(Ill. page 53)

*Encounter in Space*, (1898–99)
(GW 136)
Coloured woodcut, 190 x 252 mm
NG.K&H.A.19103
(Ill. page 55)

*Winter*, (1899)
Oil on cardboard, 60.5 x 90 cm
Unsigned
NG.M.00570. Bought in 1901
(Ill. page 57)

*Dance of Life*, 1899–1900
Oil on canvas, 125 x 191 cm
Signed lower left: E. Munch 99, top right:
E. Munch 1900
NG.M.00941. Gift from Olaf Schou in 1910
(Ill. page 59)

*The Girls on the Bridge,* (1901)
Oil on canvas, 136 x 125 cm
Signed lower left: E. M
NG.M.00844. Gift from Olaf Schou in 1909
(Ill. page 61)

*The Kiss IV,* (1902)
(GW 204)
Two-colour woodcut, 471 x 476 mm
NG.K&H.A.19517
(Ill. page 63)

*Vampire II*, 1902
(GW 41)
Lithograph and coloured woodcut,
385 x 553 mm
NG.K&H.A.18996
(Ill. page 65)

*The Fairytale Forest,* (1901–02)
Oil on canvas, 79 x 106.5 cm
Signed lower right: Edv. Munch
NG.M.02237. Gift from Alfred Larsen in 1950
(Ill. page 67)

*The Brooch. Eva Mudocci*, 1903
(GW 244)
Litograph, 605 x 474 mm
NG.K&H.B.00816
(Ill. page 69)

*Self-Portrait*, 1905
Watercolour and pastel on cardboard,
44 x 41.5 cm
Signed top right: E Munch 1905
NG.M.01229. Bought in 1921
(Ill. page 77)

*Man in the Cabbage-Field*, 1916
Oil on canvas, 136 x 180 cm
Signed lower left: E. Munch 1916
NG.M.01865. Gift from Charlotte and Christian
Mustad 1937
(Ill. page 71)

*Bathing Man,* (1918)
Oil on canvas, 160 x 110 cm
Unsigned
NG.M.01699. Gift from the artist in 1927
(Ill. page 73)

*Autumn Ploughing*, 1919
Oil on canvas, 110.5 x 145.5 cm
Signed lower right: E. Munch 1919
NG.M.01863. Gift from Charlotte and Christian
Mustad 1937
(Ill. page 12)

*Self-Portrait with the Spanish Flu*, 1919
Oil on canvas, 150 x 131 cm
Signed top left: Edv. Munch 1919
NG.M.01867. Gift from Charlotte and Christian
Mustad 1937
(Ill. page 75)